Shivoham

Poems of Spirituality,

Politics

and Human Descent.

Gopi Warrier and Jesus Fullman ©

Acknowledgements

To Pankaj Talwar, my wife Chotu,
close friend and associate Sarah Morritt,
Christina Lenz,
Kamala Jassal, Pallavi Gunwant,
the late Srikanta Datta Narasimha Raja Wadiyar;
to my partners and friends for over forty years
David McAlpine and Michael Thorpe, and
to poet Michael Woods, and all those who have
supported Delhi London Poetry Foundation
so much for over thirty five years
without whose help we would not be here.

Credits:

Sarah Morritt for layout of text, editing,
photography and design of the book cover.

Pallavi Gunawant and Kamala Jassal
for administrative support.

Adolf von Bernd: For book cover detail
from painting "Heavenly Organ"

Printed and bound by CMP (uk) Limited I www.cmp-uk.com

Polite Notice from Delhi London Poetry Foundation.

It has recently been brought to the attention of Delhi London Poetry
Foundation that some poems, films and ideas have been copied.
All our poets' work is subject to copyright, and of the
code of decency which all poets of integrity always respect.

VARAHA THE SECRET OF EVOLUTION

by Gopi Warrier

Published by Mayur University, London.

"This is one of the most unusual collection of poems I have come across for a long time.
Gopi Warrier's poetry reminds me of Kahlil Gibran, Baudelaire, and Ramakrishna Paramahamsa - prophetic, passionately sensual deeply personal, spiritual and revelationary.

Prophetic as in Gibran's writing, passionate as Baudelaire and spiritual as Ramakrishna Paramahamsa.
The English poet Alexander Pope also comes to mind with his scathing criticism of British society as in Warrier's poems called 'Indian Socialites' and 'The English Middle Classes'.

Mr.Warrier obviously comes from a well- established family as is evident from his wide travels and education.

The poem I like best 'Any Takers' is a succinct analysis of the condition of the world today.
I also particularly liked the poem 'Serengeti'- which is a beautiful evocation of the power of sound and silence.

"As a child
you loved absorbed and learnt
from these gentle animals of
pre-speech autistic days
the circumference of your own silence."

Apart from the spiritual and political poems I really liked his romantic poetry which I found extremely beautiful. As a longstanding Indophile of a strong classical Hindu orientation these poems remind me very much of a Shiva-like figure longing for union with a Parvati-like Shakti in the absence of which union the world trembles and quakes into fragments every day as we are now witnessing.
As Gopi Warrier warns 'only then will the Richter stop'. How amazingly powerful and prophetic in the times that we are living in".

Professor Michael Wood: in Literature Review International .

Foreword by David McAlpine

for "Tenth Incarnation" by Gopi Warrier

"I have known Gopi Warrier as a friend and colleague for over thirty five years and it is a considerable privilege to be asked to write this foreword to his latest book of poems with the uncompromising subtitle:
"The Destruction and Transformation of the Existing World Order".

The Tenth Incarnation of Vishnu referred to in the title is none other than Kalki who incarnates during the Kali Yuga or Iron Age in which we are now living, to redeem and save those that are worthy. The Kali Yuga in Indian Philosophy is the last in the cycle of Yugas and is the one during which virtue degenerates and rulers plunder and destroy other countries.

This is a world where we literally cannot see the wood from the trees. We are totally confused by the potent effects of 'Maya' the illusory sensate world of pleasure seeking and gadgets, unwilling to recognise that much of the cultural and political infrastructure we cling to is now toxic in nature and the cause of our downfall.

If it is the duty of an artist to selflessly and bravely direct humanity toward the firm ground of truth and love, then this work is a prime example.

This book is scathing about the sham of the so-called 'International Community' consisting as it does of just the US, France and Britain whose leaders have been all too ready to bomb thousands of women and children in African and Asian countries in the name of 'democratisation.'

In 'Eating Humble Pie', politicians' shallow motives are contrasted with the deaths they have caused.

"Politicians must eat humble pie
with different ingredients to others -
of lost elections, drowned majorities
leaving Downing Street in tears,
with their wives in tow
weeping loud not for the souls of those
killed by their husbands in illegal wars,
but for their lost aura of
power and patronage."

I believe this book of poems as well as others by Gopi can help to influence people toward the true purpose of life, long acknowledged in both Western and Eastern philosophy, which is to attain self-realisation and liberation while acting selflessly for the benefit of humanity.

Even if only a handful of people are assisted to set out on this path it will have achieved its purpose.

David McAlpine, Publisher.
Delhi London Poetry Foundation

David has lived all over the world particularly in Europe and South America as his father was a senior British diplomat.
He is a scion of the McAlpine Construction Company in the UK.

Devi Mahatmya

"Yah Devi sarvabhuteshu Vishnumayena

samstitha

namostasye namostasye namostasye

namo namaha"

The Glory of the Great Goddess
To the Goddess who exists in every living being
as the power of illusion created by Vishnu.
(translation from Sanskrit verse)

Dedication

To you who converts the small beam

of my poor light into the beautiful hologram

of this illusory universe

whose soft, gentle and sometimes furious sounds

I try to make into meaningful,

sadly often angry poems,

my humble Namaskar

G.W.

Contents

Part 1: Sadhana: Liberation from Karma

Encoding in Gene

One Small Dharma in Kaliyuga

Death of Nurse in Rosenheim, Bavaria

Spiritual Obstetrics

Om

Meditation on Autumn

Absence of Pain

Katie the Storm

Caged Souls

The Lament of JC

Reincarnation of Mary Magdalene

The Karma of Jesus now Clearly in my Room

Into Priesthood

Horse and Rider

Maha Kali Dancing on Shiva

Any Takers

Saviours

Godsports

Dear Man

Shivoham

R.E.M.

Farewell

Part 2: Satwic

Innocence in a Toxic World
Masters of the Clouds
Political Philosophy of a Heron in Regent's Park
Disciple
The King Who Walked Away From War
In Praise of the English
Vishnu
Jihad
You Too are the Brahman
Singapore
Serengeti
Spirit Taxi
The Beginning of Love
The Woman That You Love
Swastika
Trapeze
I Ammmmm
The Breath of the Shining Skull

Part 3: Rajasic

Less Grammar More Counsel

King Kumbuka of Regent's Park

The Work of John

Eating Humble Pie

Six Opinions on Freedom of Speech

The W.A.S.P's Nightmare

The Art Con

Quexit

At a Carnatic Music Concert in Madras

Forty

Taking Breaths

One Man's Empire

Insignificance

Writing a Poem

Autumn on the Hills of Jouy-En-Josas

Where Kalki Rides

The Destruction of Tripura

Part 4: Tamasic

Definitions of Terror
Stop This War
The VicTory Party
An Indian Fashion Show
Indian Socialites
Then Spain, Now Iraq
NATO Foreign Policy
International Community
British Values
A Brat is Born
Grate Britain
Transmigration Desk
The Good the Sad and the Ugly

Sadhana: Liberation from Karma.

Sadhana is the life of seekers.

Of constant awareness of their thoughts, actions and feelings,
and of spiritual practice where nothing else matters
other than transcendence from the karma which
brought one back into the illusion of this world – the
hologrammic projection of a three dimensional universe
constructed from a flat two dimensional plane
of light and darkness, from which
the three gunas Satwic, Rajasic and Tamasic
create our three dimensional illusion.

Encoding in Gene

Just a red blob
on the spine of a tadpole
few centimetres long
our heart arrived here
pushed from a mother's womb
swimming through a million years
of our karma.

Brave Valentina Tereshkova
by mistake pushed a button
sending her further up in space
not back to earth

brought down finally
decoding a program
in a flimsy wooden Sputnik
burnt by space.

Our heads arrived here on Earth
pushed out by mothers in space,
encoding in charred genes
million lives of family karmas
scripting for each
a domestic drama.

One Small Dharma in Kaliyuga

To slip ten pounds
into the hands of an old man
sitting on a park bench
looking unkempt, lonely, homeless,
thinking, feeling, knowing he is a failure when
he does not expect or ask for it
is warm, gentle satisfaction in a crass world.

When he accepts it,
whether with a nod, a handshake,
just a quick grab, a "thanks guv",
a song or even a blown kiss
one is grateful he took it,
poor, yet unresentful, who,
like so many, sluice gates open,
now sadly flood the streets and parks everyday
of this large city stinking
of ill-gotten wealth.

Dharma not to be done
as an exercise in jogging or cycling one's ego
into others walking,
but devoid of drama,
only path to liberation
in this unamusing park called Kaliyuga.

The Death of a Nurse in Rosenheim, Bavaria

for Christina Lenz

She was born in Triers
with a blessing from Trinity.

They moved to Rosenheim, Bavaria
in hearing distance of sad prayers of
the old Benedictine Pope, scholar now recluse.
Her mother a nurse in intensive care, father an architect.

Christina, too became a healer of people, cranial osteopath.
Murmurs in peoples' brains told her hands
where to find pain and how to heal them,
even feared suicidal migraines, clusters of headaches.
In the divine architecture of brain she saw pain
differently from doctors of neurology.

Then her mother had brain cancer,
several operations, for three years dreading death,
screaming in fear every night,
Christina sat by her sometimes injecting morphine
for pain, calming her fear.

After screaming continuously for a week
the mother died at 7am on a May morning,
Christina at her side, like the great Sage Shankara,
chasing the demons of death scaring her.

She died peacefully, smiling.
Christina said she heard angels sing up above and
bells ring gently when her mother breathed her last.

A rationalist would say she just wished hard
to hear such welcome.
Sceptical about Christian heaven and angels
I still believe her.
That she willed contours in the cosmic brain,
partly her own, stronger than brains of humans in pain,
she, cranial osteopath, to produce beautiful music
welcoming her poor old mother.

Almost as proof the doctor who arrived
an hour later to produce the death certificate
was a sweet, angelic nun.
It was like telling her
"your mother has indeed now
arrived in heaven"

Or was it sweet Angela,
singing for the German soul
now sin free, to be let in?

Spiritual Obstetrics

No obstetrician guarantees
live birth of a baby.
Hence the happiness as they hear the cry
after the slap on the bottom.

Only the Brahman sees
the illusory foetus of a universe
in his own REM sleepy mind
brings it out seemingly alive
but in reality just theatre
of slapping those who deserve it
for a poor last performance

Remember the Brahmin who lost eight children
in birth and came to Krishna but received no succour?
Krishna knew his karma and of the unborn child,
a sage, not meant to suffer a world again.

Egotistic Arjuna stepped in, vowed to save
the next child with his own life,
but the foetus was taken
even before birth, from the wife's womb.

Every human birth is pre-ordained
beyond the ego I, V
as poor Gandhari learnt from the dead foetus
in vitro, slipped with butter in jars
turning into hundred tamasics.
Thanks but no thanks to grateful Vyasa's obstetrics,
Kurukshetra was won only with Krishna's tricks.

Om

Only

breath Om

taste Om

touch Om

hear Om

speak Om

Live

hearts filled with Om

brains lit by Om

to find true liberation.

There is no other way

other than fleeting joys of

a million sorrow filled lives.

A Meditation on Autumn in Regent's Park

You said this is the autumn of your life
as we walked through the park,
your jacket and your hair the colour
of autumn leaves,
your fragile face and tired eyes still beautiful
and sad at the passing of years.

Autumn of our body is
Spring of the spirit and the soul
of which the body is only carrier.

Souls have no autumn or winter
but rests only in eternity
till it finds its way back there
through this giant park
we think is amusement.

Yet I must hold your hand tight
for the remaining rides.

Absence of Pain

Absence of pain
is more blissful
than presence of pleasure

All pleasure in this world
whether wine, women or wealth
ends in pain.

Pain is prarabdha karma
most difficult to break from.

The knowledge it too must pass one day
spiritual methylation of gene,
detachment from ego
feeding on pleasure

the determination never
to come back here, ever again,
is freedom.

Katie the Storm

Appearance of Jesus before the Storm Easter Sunday 2016

The storm ambled in like an old train
Gusting occasional steam,
half the compartments empty,
others full, spilling wind,
pushy commuter on the platform
of this vast city.

With Katie (also named Rosslyn,
as the chapel of Magdalene)
came the troubled soul of her lover,
unannounced, into my sole wind proof room.
Soul's wind proof room.

It is 6.00 pm on Easter Sunday.
I see the tortured face of Jesus
screwed up in the pain of crucifixion
below the hook formed by a telephone wire,
as though it's a choice between
death on the cross or suicide.
Mere cellophane twisted into a face
in severe pain crying out on a carrier bag
named "Game of Thrones."
More the Crown of Thorns.
"Isusova Kruna"

Why today I wonder?
His repetitive challenge to my contempt
for the Resurrection fable about him
who died in India, much later, his Virgin birth?
Or his third and final plea for help
to reveal the truth,
persecuted by the false faith in his name
that still binds him,
seeking escape from the karma of
crusades, the holocaust,
to the spiritual decadence and collapse
of cultures which so naively conceived him
as their 'Son of God'?

Or simply an old photograph,
a selfie, 'carrying'
abandoned Yasodhara,
Buddha's endemic pain
from another lifetime ?

Caged Souls

Walking by the zoo in Regent's Park
see a giant cross in a fish net -
hear singing in the background.

Puzzled.
This must be
Jesus Christ Superstar
matinee in the park, open air.

Walking closer it is a bird cage
supported by a cross-like
giant piece of wood
holding the net upright.

How appropriate.
Thought of poor birds –
so many caught and imprisoned
by the Cross and the fishnet
caged here for ever on Earth
like poor JC himself.

Let him, let them, fly,
let them free
from hollow stories,
empty churches,
to find their own salvation.

The Lament of J.C.

After four hours on the Cross,
I fall, as planned, still conscious.
Magdalena now M
tends me with sensual care, taking part,
as she always did, in that ultimate deception.

She applies commiphora to my bleeding wounds
and covers my face with her voluptuous body so that
none can see my gratitude. The Roman soldiers
look at her contemptuously with lust.

I think, in opiate daze, of
how badly I have treated her.
How I cursed and rebuked her for pleasure she took
from men from whom she took money to feed me.
My jealousy at her encounters was sharp
and pitiless though I depended on them.
Her residual longing for shopkeepers
and other men of petty means,
when she is now a Princess once baffled me -
but that was how she fed us all then, though
she and I kept the others guessing.

It was a relief not to die
and fun to play the game of miracles

I blessed Magdalena that all she wished
and prayed for would come true.
Here I am now using her prayers
as I did her body once, for love and sustenance.

I never thought that the Cross will one day become
an icon of torture and oppression
to spell the death of a culture that helped me
live through the Crucifixion, and then
received me and protected us for fifty years.

That the mantras I learnt at the feet of the Nath masters,
on which I meditated on the Cross,
will be reviled by missionaries bearing my name.
That the mountains that gave me refuge
will be torn apart along a line drawn
by a drunken British General in a fit of pique.
That six million will be killed
for the crime of killing me who never died.
I taught forgiveness and claimed resurrection.
Ha! I cannot but laugh in self-contempt
at those monstrous lies I helped create.

From each Jew I see I seek forgiveness
with each breath I fight the myth
from whose retaliating karma forms my stigmata.

In Germany my soul shudders with electric fright
at a darkness I comprehend as the evil from my own untruth.

I now roar
like the thunderbolt of Indra
armed with the trident of Shiva
Aghora and the Sudarsana.

These missiles must and will be launched
if the charade does not stop,
if the Satan of the West
keeps using my name to put their
greedy and rapacious hands on cultures
where there are still sacred truths,
where real Gods and Goddesses still play
and manifest their power.
I have become one with them.
I do not know my face,
but I know
the armour that I wear.

The Reincarnation of Mary Magdalene

Of course we were married.
Secretly, in that gnostic temple
in the Jewish ghetto.
I still wear the mark of that thick ring
from a birth two thousand years ago,
the only real stigmata.

I saved you from that Cross with the labour
of my body that Pilate loved and you
willingly shared, knowing that it suited us all.
It's true Judas betrayed you and
they tried to crucify you.
But Pilate and I had agreed
you would be taken off the Cross,
after a kerchief of opium made you faint
as though dead, from the loss of blood
from the Crucifixion.

It was I and Mary your mother,
who took you to the cave where you lay,
badly though not fatally wounded, for three days,
then to get up well with fiction that you rose from the dead
"Son of God"!

I played along with it all as I loved you so deeply
for what you gave me that no-one had.
Love, respect for the good you saw in me,
and your need for my love when others wanted only
my breasts, thighs and their brief minutes of passion
away from nagging wives.

When you "resurrected"
as your disciples so cleverly called it,
in fear of discovery, you wanted to leave Judea
immediately, and for me to stay on.
Pilate wanted me at least once a week
and you were afraid he will stop us both.

It was then that you promised me
you will never abandon me
and asked me to stay back till you,
and Mary, whom you could not leave behind,
reached a safe haven in far-away Kashmir
where you had once been.
You promised you will send Thomas to take me
back to you with our two children.
I was carrying your second child.
You wouldn't even take the first, named after John,
who you knew had always been stronger,
more learned in the occult arts and powerful,
not deterred even in death.

Then you left suddenly at midnight
without even a proper goodbye.
Just a warm affectionate hug, but no sorrow in your eyes
as though you were now just leaving the prostitute,
not your wife and the mother of your children,
your protector and your local bank,
I never rejected a single request.

May be it was just your defence against hurt.
May be it was just you.
I never heard from you again.

Your disciples made you into God, the Son of God,
all the accolades you dreamt of but never enjoyed.
That was your Karma that continues to this day
where you are now always a stranger in
someone else's land, despised foreigner as
you were then, hating this religion in your name
for it couldn't be more false, all this nonsense
about "Virgin Birth" and "Only Son of God".
Like that of blind-folded Gandhari on noble Krishna,
my sorrow follows you.

The curses of six million Jews
killed in the holocaust haunt you
and hold you back from your own liberation
let alone your saving others –
your sad hunted face, and that of Mary,
keeps appearing to Sages beseeching them,
pleading for release.

All that you now touch turns to ash.
You cry for that religion that took you in
which foolish Evangelists destroy,
as they have done in Chile, Peru –
of that glorious culture,
a giant cross for you to carry now.

You suffer breathlessness,
your ribs hurt with costochondritis
and your neck is twisted with three cervical vertebrae
slipping each time a Christian priest
offers a healing in your name.

You have no home. No money left.
You have no purpose having learnt
that life is not what you preached,

that you can offer no-one redemption from sin.
Your soul is trapped in this horrible world
unless the so-called Christians
understand your plight and release you.

For what I did,
none of it bad in the eyes of the real God,
I was born a Princess again and again.

My children ruled over Europe
till their descendants became evil
with the self-same theology to buttress them,
and when thrown out in revolutions,
their children became corrupt politicians
waging wars only for money, from sale of arms
or the popular vote, never mind the millions
killed in your name for their greed.

But I too, like you,
for my part in that lie
still traverse this world
seeking my escape.

The Karma of a Jesus now Clearly in my Room

I always liked pink shirts –
English makes – Gieves and Hawkes,
not so much Pinks,
not in silk but in cotton.

On the pink silk fabric
behind my eight Ganapathys
is a small picture of Shiva's family

including Shastha from his liaison
with Vishnu as Mohini - male Gods making love
for a cosmic victory - creating Shastha
to kill the Demoness Mahishi,
being blessed she cannot be killed
by child born of woman.

Next to this and the large picture of Krishna,
on the silk there now appears clearly
the face of Jesus, thick eyebrows,
intelligent Jewish eyes, aquiline nose,
large forehead, handsome face,
almost matted hair and beard.
Why is He here?

Is it in approval of my poem
that seeks relief for him from the Karma
of a supposed resurrection that never place,
but led to Kashmir,
the land of the Lost Tribe of Israel?
His spiritual father Shiva himself
in the land of Krishna.

Is it His soul, as that of Mary,
seeking final peace from further incarnations,
troubled by a pestilential Church –
a constant fleece on the powers of
His blood, spirit and bones?

Or is it to tell me in consternation
"look mate – I'm one of them you pray to,
stop bugging me and those who hugged me close".
Or is it simply a visit out of curiosity
from another lifetime?

Or is it the face of He who became
a voluptuous She this lifetime,
her face imprinted
on the bosom of my pink shirt
where I hug her close.

Into Priesthood

for Francois Baumann

You had everything
A degree from HEC,
good connections. Charm.

Was it the way egotistical Oriel
left you for the Schlumberger chap
that made you take
the final plunge?

Or was it the talk
of coming deluge?

In any case, Francois,
you were too good, too soft a boy
for any single girl to fully own.

Though I wonder how
you'll resist your fondness
for the steak tartare
and winter in Kitzbühel.

HEC : École des Hautes Etudes Commerciales,
France's Grande École for Management Studies.

Horse and Rider

I found the plastic horse by
Bombay Brasserie in South Kensington,
our favourite haunt those days.

A minute later it was you who found the rider
like one of the four horsemen
of the apocalypse.
He fitted perfectly on my horse.

Over many lunches at BB and Hurlingham
we perfected our objective
in code wwwc.om
beyond the power of enigmas.

One afternoon Bejoy, our favourite waiter
carried the heavy new Shiva into the car,
then home to keep Uma company by
the horseman we called Kalki.

After 30 years
the same horse
and same rider
are still on the mantel piece
but now riding close to another:
Shiva dancing cosmic dissolution.

Maha Kali Dancing on Shiva.

Maha Kali, Tripura Bhairavi
you stand astride Shiva,
your legs wide apart,
tongue dripping with blood,
all life symbolised
in the human head in your hand,
your eyes gleaming with pride
that you defeated
the Great Shiva himself.

The head in your hand
ejects a stream of blood
into your mouth
in the act of re-creation.

But Shiva has had the last laugh,
as it is not him that you killed,
but the world of Maya he willed you to,
death of the universe itself
the only way, you, Prakriti,
will join him in the eternal cycle
of the Brahman.

Any Takers

This is not the first, as some say,
but the second concluding part of Kaliyuga.

Thirty per cent will self-destruct
or be destroyed by others.

Another thirty will mutate
male to female, man to insect.

Twenty per cent will transform
over many lifetimes.

The last twenty will find liberation -
seeking it beyond this life.

This is my prediction,
I put the odds in favour a trillion to one.

Any takers?

Meet me not at Ascot
but in the betting caves
on the foothills of Kailash –
where the Sages
routinely place their bets
on the survival of mankind.

Saviours

In this zero-hour of the city,

when the moon refuses to shine

when I stand beside

the widowed sea

soliciting suicide from me

they come to me,

the galley slaves,

riding the blue.

Godsports

Anima, unseen,
under cover of darkness
you have come back
into my heart.

In my sleep's darkness
in the singularity of void
you crept inside this dusty pied-à-terre
long vacated by desire
carving a perfect citadel
for Cosmic Being,
who once judged
Eternal Dharma on earth,
far above mortal lives
and their sad inevitable karmas.

These Gods too
have now left the world
below you in pitch darkness.

Anima, as time undulates
under vertebrae of unborn stars
and galaxies collapse,
I will wake up in Ananda Tandava
the dance of ultimate bliss
as you become me.

Dear Man

Dear Man,
for cash, for love, even for pleasure,
you kill and tear each other
as only you can.

As millions of Universes
past and present span
infinite space, you,
no bigger than a fleck of ash
swagger on a speck of land
called Earth.

The size of an ant,
your legs caught in the sand
of your karma
of birth and rebirth.

I watch you with a sad glance
under the calm of the crescent moon.
With regret,
I must now begin
my Final Dance.

A Poem for Theresa

You share the birth day of a Saint,
like you also October born.
I have never met you but I see in your
large expressive eyes
the love for your good father
whom you lost suddenly, so sadly

your love for colour in your shoes,
"revealing" clothes a Libran challenge
for strict faith against parental love

and the sadness in your lips
that gurns in hypoglycaemic pain
from insulin at question time
as lunch is delayed, and your eyes and lips
search for the right feeling as you speak

But most of all I see in your eyes a gentleness
despite the bravado and anger of politics
and your love of "God" be it Jesus Christ
or the great Shiva himself.

As you look splendidly golden in your saree, eyes
reverential despite your fear and reserve in the
ancient temple of Someshwara in Bangalore, a Libran city.

Shivoham, Shivoham,
finally we are all Shiva
not sinners but
pure and eternal
consciousness.

Shivoham

Shivoham Shivoham
aham nirvikalpam

We are formless,
a product of light playing
on a flat plane of dark energy,

our ego the only character
on a flat television screen
we watch avidly
fragments of light play
versions of fake reality.

That same light inside us
watching every thought
and feeling compassion
despite knowing
it's a mere illusion,
then,

then alone,

detached from conflicts of duality

blissful

we become Shiva.

R.E.M.

God's sleep is the dream
of our existence.
Neurons of his dream crackle
an explosion of galaxies.
The birth of life is imminent,
in the next rapid eye movement.

In his dark body, as he sleeps
a white lotus creeps up
from the right atrium
into the throat.

He should soon awake,
glowing in pure consciousness.

This dream will cease.

Farewell

For Srikanta Datta Narasimha Raja Wadiyar of Mysore

The Ultimate Mantra is
beyond dark energy,
beyond sound,
beyond soundlessness,
merging nothingness.

The Ultimate Being is
without sorrow
beyond Godspots,
beyond Big Bangs,
not becoming Brahman but in
the breath of Infinite Universes
the Brahman becoming
one pulsating nothingness.

*Written on the morning of 12th December 2013
by Gopi Warrier, on the death the previous night
of his dear friend Srikanta Datta Narasimha Raja Wadiyar,
who, although born the Maharajah of Mysore, preferred
to be called just Mr Wadiyar when India so appropriately
became a Republic. He was shorn of all the appendages
of a monarch and gave many of his palaces
to the Government of India.*

Gopi Warrier.

The Satwic attributes:

People of Satwic nature are of a noble orientation,

to whom truth and compassion to others,

matter more than their own materialistic attainments,

often more than their own happiness.

Satwic people are those involved in yoga,

spiritual practice and compassionate professions

like medicine, nursing and charitable foundations

without ego and self-projection.

Innocence in a Toxic World

Three little school girls in green uniforms
of the Marylebone Church school,
walking behind me on Marylebone Road.

One said "she is creepy",
probably of a classmate.

Still ahead, still walking, I heard her comment.
Just to tease them I repeated loudly
as though to myself, "she is creepy".

They heard it and ran fast, giggling,
to catch the red London bus
arriving at Harley Street,
green uniforms fluttering in the wind.

They had no smart phones.
There is still some innocence
in a toxic world.

Masters of the Clouds

In 1400 Incas were masters of the clouds.
Sowing crops at altitudes above the Alps,
playgrounds for Europe's worthless skiing glitterati,
ignorant how sacred mountains are,
how, God-like, they protect and destroy.
Even Kailash they contaminate with ego.
Shiva, meditating, doesn't need
your dollars of rubbish.
Don't disturb him
and provoke an avalanche.

Incas too were happy.
Mythically linked to past,
aware of precise movement of planets
and a cosmos that deciphered
a purpose for their existence .

Then, of course, European Christians landed,
carrying the Cross to convert and conquer.

Fortresses and myths destroyed,
sad-eyed and bleak-faced,
the Incas now carry the Cross
for a civilisation lost forever.
Except for Western academics and
camera crew carcass feasting.

Political Philosophy of a Heron in Regent's Park

for Livingstone and Corbyn

I asked the Heron whom I knew for long
in Regent's Park, in strict confidence, "Tell me,
do you also, like the Swan, belong to the Queen?"
Standing on one leg, meditating, an old sage,
a Rabbi with a yarmulke, he snorted, laughing,
making clear he chose to speak only
as we were friends, met every day as fellow meditators
in a world going mad and said,

"What? Me!?
I don't belong to anyone
let alone a British Queen!
See my skull cap.
See the deep gash from an iron rod
of the SS Guard at Auschwitz.
I am a Socialist and a Republican.

I travel a world without no-fly zones.

I fish for souls not bomb like drones.
I have no boundaries of class, colour, race,
or country, this Second Time.
I fly in peace over both Gaza and Israel.
Now let's get back to our mantras
for mankind's emancipation."

"Thank you dear Guru" I said and sat quiet, obedient.

Disciple

A thin film of a teardrop

that didn't fall

in your eyes

as you watched me prostrate

to your gentle and serene Guru.

Your gratitude for my respect,

love for his care over the years

that saw your fortunes swing from millions

to the verge of bankruptcy, suicide.

I love you

for that surrender.

The King Who Walked Away from War

King Ashoka, disciple of Buddha, renounced war
and walked away from conquest's sorrow, his empire,
even the illusion of a Universe.

For the self-indulgent, egotistical, upstart West
Universe exists for conquest.
Proclamations of war not peace define nationhood.
Grand stand, punch above one's weight,
act a great power but can't feed or house one's own poor.
Death is for foot soldiers, 'infidels' or any 'other'
whose land holds oil, gold or wastes to dump convicts
and lower classes, for whose salvation
yob princes and fake duchesses are paraded.

Anglo Saxons love whisky, wars, wardrobes and women –
in that order. Except for the Minister,
arms-dealers and secret agents, who love money.
War, arms deals and embedded media hype
to declare it, is big business.
The French, latecomers, make a killing in Libya
big enough to launch a Hedge Fund.
Le Bouffon Francais d'alma mater invades Mali
in amorous grandeur.

The Church worships Crusaders
carrying the Cross to conquer and convert.
"Turbulent priests" and Popes in fancy dress,
who once 'heiled Hitler' and 'blessed' the holocaust,
now wave incense, ring bells, kiss books, light candles,
wanting more wars to protect from 'conversion'
'primitives' they once 'saved'
only to traffic as nuns and choir boys.

Goebbels giggles at The See's conferences
on 'Trafficking' and sly 'Inculturation'.
If Pope Pius had had his way
Hitler would be canonised in a casket,
bones becoming relics for demonic worship
to curse Church enemies, casting more spells
to "double, double, toil and trouble."
England's Green Man, gentle pagans
and 'witches' the Church burnt at stake
only to steal a peaceful religion from,
will strike back. Forsooth!
Invaders, incantating priests, politicians,
even poor refugees, suffer inevitable karma.

They brutally behead.
We destroyed Iraq,
killed in Ferguson and Tottenham.
Others thousands in Palestine and Ukraine.
Two anti-goddess cults, one with 'His 'fable' colonising,
other with Her name, abducting 160 now
not 16 in absurd 'heaven.'

Echoes in Europe of Third Reich
as poor Muslims are spat upon, reviled.
"Sweet Helen, for love of thee instead of Troy
shall Wittenberg be sacked?"
Leaders need Sages and Philosophers
not Caplins or Ritalin.

Next Christmas it is Buddha who must speak:
You have done enough damage to this world.
I walked away from a kingdom.
Be brave, walk away from war.

In Praise of the English

For Boris and fellow MPs

"Tuck your shirt in" they tell Boris,
his tails flapping in Parliament –
affectionate schoolboys prodding
a naughty fool into mischief.

Whatever the faults of Brits
they make loyal friends,
have great courage and are originals –
not replays of some American dream.

The love of an English rose is gentle,
yet wildly sensual,
in betrayal is jealous rage.
Her breasts are soft and
her heart responds to tenderness.

A well-bred Englishman will give
his life and even go to prison for you.
For him the difference between
Eton and Wormwood Scrubs
is marginal, as for a school of tramps
moving from one Garden Square
to another in London.

But it is difficult to penetrate
an English heart
so caught up in posturing
and in such undue loyalty
to dustbins in Sandringham,
and spoilt brats who suck the blood
of deference from this Nation.
The charade of divine right and fading pomp
keeps the loyalty of this nation
so narrowly between the seas
of a no longer 'sceptred isle'.

The English spirit will no longer fly
unless its mascot dies a natural death
like any other soap opera -
from public boredom.

England does not need a King
when every English home is castle.
England needs no Queen when
every English woman demands
the devotion of Queens.

The poor and the lower class
have the heart and the art
to reunite this nation,
but its blood must flow through
Republican veins not tainted
Saxburg-Gotha ones.

Vishnu

Vishnu means the All-Pervasive One.
We are all Vishnu,
you, me and you.
Some for all the time to some,
others for some time to all.

But none all the time to all,
including the Gods themselves,
whose devotees are even
more fickle than lovers
as they simply, greedily,
want and want,
and switch Gods and prayers
like they do banks,
loans, and overdrafts.

Jihad

The ultimate form
is dark energy,
formlessness.
Sankara calls it
"Nirvikalpa"
as in Chidambara Rahasya
where the "secret" is
nothingness.

In its refusal of imagery
perhaps Islam got it right.
Rama and Shiva happily co-exist.
Peace and Jihad are simply
states of mind.

Jihad means bliss and
nothingness.

You Too Are the Brahman

Driving through Baker Street, London,
a Nigerian taxi driver, an Ibo,
always super intelligent,
respectfully asked me today
what the real basis of Hindu religion was,
how he had thought the Hindus so moral
and well behaved, could be so Pagan in belief,
worshipping millions of Gods.

On a whim, I compared the car he was driving
to the Universe, how each part was essential,
some much more than others –
the wheels which moved the car
were Brahma, the Creator
who kept Universes going forward
through good and bad roads.

Vishnu, the Preserver, was the engine
that made the car fulfil its purpose,
the substratum of every Universe.

Shiva the exhaust, the smoke, destroyed
particles of the carbon monoxide of our illusion -
that our ego's upward mobility is good for all.

That all cars must one day stop,
so He has space for His Final Dance, and Shakti,
the fuel, the female energy
without which the car, the Universe,
is just an empty shell.

All other Gods were each part of the car
each with a purpose, some essential, some not,
windscreen wipers only in rain,
lights at night, fog horns only on the Alps.
Warrior Gods when wars must be won.

"Isn't there then an ultimate God,
just one, like Jehovah?"
the intelligent driver asked again.
I said yes, of course,
it is You, Yourself,
the driver your Soul,
your will, one with the Gods,
who makes the game of the Universe possible,
and others like you without whom
the car of the universe
can never move.

I am the Brahman – Aham Brahmasmi -

but you too are the Brahman.

Singapore

A poem for Ken Barber

Most accountants are boring.
You were a Che Guevara
almost a non- governmental institution,
forty years helping us
small, cash strapped businessmen
Charities 'duck and dive,' as you used
to say with that twinkle in your eyes,
from Government militias,
tax collectors, prosecutors and
worst of all the bailiffs
who chuck their meagre possessions
on waiting lorries.

You had great flair too
not just in your golf drive
but the greeting cards you chose
for your charity enterprise
that made the millions you never
sought yourself.

But why Singapore?
Why did you dream of Singapore so much?
You always wanted to go there.

You said, with that same
twinkle in your eye,
But that it was the one thing
you always wanted to do in your life.

I promised I would take you there
if we ever hit the big time,
slush with funds.

Then you became ill.
We went bust.
Even after your op you helped us
and many others for little,
mostly nothing.

Today I hear you died.
I am sad I could never take you
to Singapore.

But I know for sure
you are somewhere where
your credits are far far more
than your liabilities.

Serengeti

Anuradha,
as usual you flee speechless,
an antelope in the vast and beautiful
plains of Serengeti.
Your large eyes impersonate
fear of approaching lions,
but there is no pride, only a herd of elephants
led by your own son, Ganapathy
born from your body's dust,
elephant-head Shiva given,
merely seeking play with you.

As a child you loved, absorbed and learnt from
these gentle animals of pre-speech autistic days,
the circumference of your own silence.
You came before as Parvati
from this very part in Gondwana
as continental drift, feet first,
and touched me as a mountain.

You took your companion bird
from the crest of Kilimanjaro,
and having dropped your third breast
on the coast of Zanzibar at Unguja,
floated fast as a landmass to Kailash,
the Meru and to me.

All because you had heard
in your left ear the word,
the word that was God,
Omkara,
primal mantra of Veda,
secret link of man's evolution from monkey.
Om is fire, light, the word that triggers
Mooladhara's move to man in the Kundalini,

Even now you find speech difficult,
let alone talking of love.
Pre Vedic priests still use your
genetically encoded bird sound in ritual.

Families are only fellow passengers on red buses
changed at the bus stops of lifetimes
but your Dharma remains in each incarnation
sacrosanct, to be fulfilled
or carried on enfeebled shoulders,
as time passes and yugas weaken.

Each day you are away, foolishly, another bomb
will drop, people die, the governments fall,
shares collapse and banks flop –
the aftermath of each rejection.

Anuradha, understand -
only when I am inside you
will the richter stop.

Spirit Taxi

A Poem for Mike

You had left your past behind,
became an engineer, an MBA
from the best business school ,
broke through the class barrier
unashamed of your past, unlike others
whose parents were working class.
You were secretly proud of your father,
a Leo,who retired as a plumber but
remained staunchly working class
unflinching against apologetic turncoats
who still tugged forelocks.

Your wife the nutritionist
gently teased you and your father,
now a widower, about his set ways,
but you always took his side,
sometimes on my advice
as I too admired his spirit.

He became ill. Badly constipated
with a cancer of the bowel
he refused to operate.

You told me how he struggled in pain
to defecate, and clawed at the faecal matter in him,
and you, without hesitation, helped him dig it out
with your bare hands from his back passage.
That is what I call love
and the highest compassion.

Then he died one afternoon.
I had to come and see you that night.

My driver took me to a friend's house
from where I took a taxi, as your house
was impossible to find at night
through the villages of Hertfordshire.
The old taxi driver was exceptionally nice to me –
almost affectionate, as though he knew me before,
whizzed me straight to your house
through narrow roads
without a question, and waited
a few yards from your door.

When I came out
he flashed his head-lights
in friendly recognition.
As he came near I asked you
if his face was familiar.
You said "Yes, he was a replica"
of your father.

The Beginning of Love

Deep within the indestructible self's
powerful diamond core
nothing exists other than pure light
and though nothing enters there
alone you have reached my soul.

The past is a mercurial flow into the present.
The lives we lived before fall into
and softly fill the crevices between us.
Pain explains itself in this mirror –
perfect reflection of the past.

I do not understand time as you do.
For me it is always still. You define it,
thereby extend the corners of the Universe
and my spatial interjection into void,
creates each time, the new reality.
No accidental act each meeting
tracing back finally consumed in your sensuality.
ah! how precise the sukshma tantra of ordained reunion.

You once again become Durga
and with your hands in a magical trance
reverse the Germanic Swastika.
Atharvana and Advaita samskaras fuse into one –
the Cosmic force.

The Woman That You Love

The taste that you long for
is the love that you lost.
The kiss that you miss
is the look that you loved
but never came your way
till the last.

The money that you rake in,
the power that you ache for,
the bombs that you drop,
the men that you send into war,
is from a love that was faked
that still breaks your heart.

The touch that you sigh for
but never get
is the love that you dispatched
with tears in her eyes.

The woman that you love
the woman that you crave for
is the one that you cheated
and walked away from.
this is the sum of our lives.

Swastika

In this Bavarian air an electric
crackling of danger.
Here in the woods the mother
was shot or shot herself.
The daughter had to bend forward
to be taken (they said willingly) in the rear.
A military truck, red, lights subdued,
reverses into my dream.

We were Aryans
with the viral energy of Gods.
We arrived here as dust
on the edges of light from
over a million exploding Supernovae.
Particles of brightness, which like charms
had the clarity of God's kingdom though
in its soft underside our alter-ego
desired separation if not freedom.
Mutation of the protozoid
in nature and its self-destruction
was our stated goal.

For they were Aborigines,
demonic races who fell with Lucifer.

But in liberation nature herself changed,
her own image no longer immune.

Light's distortion penetrated her cellular core,
broke the mirror of her pure waters.
Now only the stench remains,
the semen rotting in plastic sheath,
wombs of a new generation.

In a red sky black letters,
occult signs, spell magic and evil –
the self-detonation of nature
by her own left hand.
She will, as intended,
have to invite dissolution,
uterus emptying into the black hole
of planetary collapse.
Is benediction a pure white snake,
rising from the gloom
of a lost species -
a civilisation for over ten thousand years?

Oh Bavaria, how I remember thee
second receptacle for the fallen soul.

I Ammmmmmm.

We were in the comfortable large
Moghul restaurant next to
London Business School in the Park
where I first came 42 years ago
then it became another haunt.

That evening with friends
a single older woman walked in
walked around the restaurant looking
at the ceiling like a council inspector

from our table I asked her what she was up to
She said this music is too loud,
India is spiritual not this disco sound.

First irritated, my heart melted
at the words 'India', 'spiritual'.
Turned out she is a Scandinavian
psychotherapist who meditates.

I asked her what she meditates on
She said "not on 'Om' - it's religious" -
Her teacher, an American,
taught her to meditate on just

" I Am"

like
I Ammmmmmmmmm,

"like 'Ommmmmmmm'
but better" he said.

I didn't have the heart to tell her
I AM nothing
OM is everything
Because I,
me,
too
am nothing.

Trapeze

In another Yuga
Sukaracharya, great Sage,
suspended himself over fire,
inhaling smoke, to save
his incendiary disciples the Asuras,
insatiably waging war
against the Gods.

All Bodhisattvas must remain on earth
said Buddha, to save each and every soul
till the bitter end.

Sages remain suspended above earth,
catching rising and falling souls
in darkness.
There is no safety net.

The clowns cry, their antics
no longer amuse the audience
of adults swapping wives.
Children beget other children
or are on cocaine or bombing raids.

Fools talk about ozone
and climate change, petty blows
on behemoth of cosmic space.

My problem is gate collection
of good souls is nil,
today and every day.
Let the circus close.

The Breath of the Shining Skull

for the Yogi and the Railway Buff

Father built this railway forty years ago.
As a train chugs up onto the wide mountains
its steam engine, like an ageing heart,
struggles valiantly, missing a puff or two.

From the vantage point of the last cabin,
the Chairman's saloon, he explains
how we could measure the speed of the train
by counting the track beat, rather like taking the pulse
of an old sherpa climbing a mountain.

At ten, I had no guilt at the comfort of the saloon,
which, with three bedrooms and more
can accommodate three hundred others travelling
on the roof of the next compartment.

The train snakes up along its mountain tracks
and into a tunnel over two miles long.
Time for an amorous but shy couple in the third class
to steal a quick kiss unseen in the dark
by prying eyes intrusive in the light.

Half an hour in the dark and the train emerges
into the blazing afternoon and steams,
stationary, on Punalar platform where

red bananas from the mountains are seen
for the first time in the journey.
The yogi calls it Kapala Bhasthi
the breath of the Shining Skull.
Like the train he puffs out hard,
each outward breath cleansing the sinuses.
After the cleansing he ejects the steam
of the 15 lettered mantra into the kundalini
and pushes it along the track to
the snow crested peak of Mount Meru,
the spine of the universe. Though still,
in the lotus mudra he moves upwards.

At the level of the throat chakra the
kundalini rests before its final ascent into the
most difficult tunnel, where Shiva and Shakti
embrace after a cosmic day's separation.
Each speck of phlegm, the smug ego of kapha
and self-orientation, perish in the exhaustion
of the fight against base nature.

There in the light of the third eye,
Shiva, Parameshwara smiles,
Vishnu - Maya burns inside and outside of him.
The skulls keep piling up.

Father was Parameshwar.
But it is I, the son, who now weaves
the garlands of skulls.

Rajasic

Rajasic attributes:

Intellectual, politically controlling and astute people
whose lives are driven by their strong ego,
professional ambition and the control
of social and personal relationships.
People who succeed in politics, business and the media.
Politicians of the Rajasic nature and strong ego
are the people who lead their countries to war.
Rajasic people don't indulge in physical violence.
They can, and often do, politically incite
violence and war in those of a Tamasic nature.

Rajasic nature can be transcended through
egoless devotion in a chosen religious path
or by selfless service to humanity.

Less Grammar, More Counsel

Two young women have the old British disease.
Inflection of accent is an infection of the 'lower class.'
They are, of course, "posh," immune from this virus.
"Posher" than their mother, a doctor.
All because they went to a private school.

They call their mother
"Council House," even "Liverpool Scum."

Comprehensive suicide
of schools of medics, scientists and architects.
Underpaid, undervalued, overworked
till they hit Harley Street. Few do.

There are far better schools than Eton
in this world, dear deluded English snobs.
Please stop the boast
"We are the greatest"
as even 'lower orders' do.
"Oh! They did win the battle of Waterloo".

Etonians are not the problem but
the easy ride grammarian wannabes
give them and royals as if
they were anything special.
A curious cocktail of servility iced with envy

in social climbers peculiar to England.
Not racist to others but classist to their poor.

This Bipolar Society badly needs lithium,
seeing twit and moron from 'historic home' or palace
as "toff , aristocrat, royal,"
but a doc or scientist as 'scum',
wants stronger medicine than Valium.

Haloperidol will certainly halt this delusion.
Sadly Parliament is already on Prozac
with strong side effects,
less libido.
But more wars for men
trying to prove their manhood.
Perhaps a small dose of ECT will do the trick.
We need a few convulsions,
more class breaking souls.

King Kumbuka of Regent's Park

After an attempted escape
you sit there like a poor slave
caught trying to run away,

head down ashamed, afraid you may not
get another meal never knowing
this wicked species who imprisoned you in
the Guantanamo of your difference
as they always do.

Better if they imprisoned
Bucking Kumbukueen your female version
and her entourage the rutting
Kumbukess, Kumbulords, Kumbuladies.

Millions in these isles
a billion worldwide would have been free,
prosperous by now but caught,
enslaved they fought,
found freedom unlike you
breaking glass ceilings in oppressor's eyes.
Renditioned into the heart of their jungles
you now, an exhibit in the park next to
fake, frozen art.

Tranquilised back in the cage poor you
celebrate with five pints of Blackcurrant Juice.
Let Kumbukess and Kumbulords
be tickled in their nether regions with
just one ohm of live white current juice?

The Work of John

Having finished the baptism of True Labour
as brave as the work of John, good and true,
you must never kneel, or let your proud head bow
to dim-witted 'monarchs' wearing blue riband
and plastic crown, screaming with such lumpen glee
when her horse wins a penny, or gleaming in her
other occupation, the pretend 'ruling' over
imaginary 'realms' of 'Commonwealth' –
the size of a shilling in the sea.

What Empire left?

So willingly are the oppressed poor made to believe
her omnipotence and that of her thuggish poseur brood.
Their praises sung by subservient God men and Lords men
in comic regalia, strutting cathedrals of abuse where
the very sins they decry they themselves enjoy secretly
from nun rape to paedophilia.

Then you were for real and I the fraud,
a crude concoction from the stories of the two Ks one
a young boy, the other the wicked king who had children
murdered in every house, searching for the child God,
transmogrified and forged as me,
and he the killer Herod.

Don't kneel, don't surrender your head to the monkeys!
But please do nationalise the railways
Stop the trains taking migrants to Nazi camps in my name.

Most importantly please privatise the 'Monarch' and progeny.
Call them B.P. Ltd but turn Buck House
into a B&B for migrants.

Let them live gloriously, not in shame,
in the zoological palace in Regent's Park,
where they belong de rigeur,
riding gear dressed, and like their relatives display
pink bottoms to their ever adoring press.

Only once you have done this, your job,
can I begin mine.

I must first disestablish that ravaging untruth
about my birth and death
still contaminating the West
for the few seekers of freedom from
this illusory universe.

I am Jesus Fullman not half man half God
but Full Man Green Man
seeking renewal of true faith,
making a haven of peace and equality
on our green and pleasant land,
until my hologrammic sleep ends her love's demand.

Eating Humble Pie

Everyone must eat humble pie,
at least once in their lives,
preferably every day.

Politicians must eat the humble pie
with different ingredients to others -
of lost elections, drowned majorities,
leaving Downing Street in tears,
with their wives in tow, weeping loud
not for the souls of those killed
by their husbands, in illegal wars,
but for their lost aura
of power and patronage.

For some a trial at The Hague
as war criminal would be an
essential ingredient to add pep to the pie.
The commissions they gained from
arms-dealers for fake wars,
and from new despots
the cent per barrel in gratitude
for the fake revolution
that put them in place,
instead of the ones before who gave
less protection money
to the International Community –

code for the Western Mafia –
should be located, seized and distributed
monthly to the asylum seekers from the
cluster-bombing and drone attacks.
Their mouths must be plastered
so we no longer hear their platitudes.

The Press and the paparazzi must
most certainly eat humble pie, being pried upon,
photographed, with paunches and wrinkles
picking up young prostitutes in Kings Cross
and being arrested occasionally,
though not jailed,
which I wouldn't wish on anyone
other than war criminals and murderers.

Bankers must eat humble pie every day,
their hedge-funds liquidated,
assets seized, their tarts unable to pay
first-class fares or jewellery from Tiffany's –
the small businesses and customers
to whom they refused credit
dancing on the embers of their arrogance.

Doctors who play truant from the NHS
to work in swish clinics in Harley Street,
charging for procedures that were really not needed,

while the poor waited in pain, on trollies in hospitals,
will and must eat the humble pie
of negligence cases, from the very same patient
whom they cheated
to buy second homes in France, -
and be disqualified from BMA.

Priests, fake gurus and healers must eat humble pie
being exposed as charlatans,
whose real interest was amassing wealth
and sexy disciples for secret assignations
that "opened their chakras" -
by losing their flock and wealth,
walking the streets,
seeking alms before salvation.

All priests who raped nuns and little boys
must be jailed and defrocked
so there is no more church.

Eating humble pie is losing the weight
of the karma, the ego,
the greed and the arrogance,
that made one strut on the stage
of a life meant to fulfil dharma,
and is the diet of the blessed, not of failure,
not to reincarnate
in the most inferior form of life,
human or otherwise.
It is only the truly evil who can never eat humble pie.

Six Opinions on Freedom of Speech:

Sages and Philosophers:

"The Ultimate Being is beyond form,
beyond 'dark energy', beyond formlessness.
Sages call it "Nirvikalpa",
infinite consciousness,
free from constraints of space,
time and timelessness.
Form is merely human ego
seeking identity in differentiation, creed."

Historians:

"The so called 'great values of Europe'
we saw in abundance seed evil
in Algeria, Asia, Africa and
the Nazi camps of Germany and Poland."

Humanists:

"State terror is infantile race ego,
upstart leaders hungering for wealth and power.
So are state executions,
fake fatal encounters without trial.
Can we ever forget Tony,
financially astute, cunning, clever
shielded by relics, rituals, Tyburn prayer."

The East:

"There were no lectures on
'civilisations clashing'
when millions were killed with a lie in Iraq,
Civilisation is not black ties at the Oscars
but spiritual sense of right dharma."

Middle East:

"Apologise for Iraq.
Leave the Middle East."

The Pope:

"Insult my mother and I will punch you in the face"

Sages and Philosophers:

"The denial of imagery is the final truth,
unseen creator formless as veiled creatrix.
True Jihad means no enemy,
no apostate, kaffir or cartoonist to kill,
only the loss of ones own ego,
ultimate bliss of nothingness.

The W.A.S.Ps' Nightmare
(How Climates Change)

They bullied every other creature,
from bees to the elephants, all petrified
of their angry sting, wild drone aggression.
The huge elephant whom they first drove mad
in Iraq fell paralysed from their crazed attack,
in 'shock and awe'.
They invented enemies and invaded any
territory where they could grab black honey
by dumping on local fauna rare Ebola and Zika
from their centres for manufacturing disease.
The money, naturally, was fenced in hedges of
Canary Wharf, Wall St. and under Panama hats
of bald bankers with botoxed wives lolling on beaches of
Bermuda and Cayman with sunburnt, withered thighs.
The wasps and the hornets
thus enslaved half the human race.

But hornets are gene recessed 'eusocial'! wasps, even more cruel.
Infesting Auschwitz, gassing caterpillars with little caps on skulls
before they emerged into art, science and beautiful music and
now shooting poison on poor migrant bees from the Mediterranean.
Wicked as Praying Mantises they preyed on their own gruesome
relics, eating ancient cultures in the fable of St. Peters' Square
pretending holiness, perfecting curses, concocting saints
to convert 'heathens' from worship of the Goddess,
the illusion of cosmos she conceives,
consciousness the only true God.

A poor man sat at that table once making 13.
Was it her? Reborn,
now the wife of one who then, sat in judgement?

Then the climate changed.
The pigs, the bulls, the elephants,
even placid cows turned against them.
Bulls charged. Elephants hooted in derision
at their shallow, deranged lives.
The pigs stopped digging for truffles
and flew away on Sundays.

Some, suckled at Bullingdon,
became Baronesses and Peers.
Pork, dead regal, in red and ermine.

Finally the Gods destroyed them for their arrogance,
flooding their nests and the queen wasp
they prized above their own servile selves,
not with arms but just words,
divine wisdom that their pride was mere illusion
their queen an old bat, not a wasp,
their President a fraud, their intelligence faked,
their religion of extracting honey from others
a selfish, evil pursuit.
The cows mooed in joy, no longer destined for burgerys.
Or shall we say "buggery," the canonisation of pædophilia
in a fake, perverted faith? Dear Wasps, (not hornets) your
nightmare is now over.
Please wake up. I am your friend.
It's time for lunch. Vegetarian?

The Art Con

"Freeze Art"! Fraud art.
Mercs cart bank tarts
round Regent's Park
as if they own it.

Press farts rate greed's warts,
the conmen, the wheelers and dealers
of the contemporary art world.

Cheap Nit Pickled Sir Otta,
social climber and pseud
please bog off to Bogota
pickled like a parotta
by Damien Hirst.

Tate Modern will have a fate
more benign without you.

Fake art, fraud art.
White Cube, plastic boob.

My poor darling Tracey Emin,
on my unmade bed,
I wake up screaming
with a nightmare dreaming
of the vermin crawling over
the body of modern art.

Quexit

If the cleaner from Southall, her daughter
an airhostess, or granddaughter the climber
becomes the President or Prime Minister
of a country without barriers, class,
caste, religion, gender or sexuality
it is a great democracy
where merit alone matters.

If the same cleaner or climber had to set out
to seduce a frog masquerading as prince,
not very bright, then becomes
a "princess" "duchess" countess and
all that stupid jazz - such medieval crap,

and a public tranquilised by
Downton needs a queen to suckle
through otherwise pathetic lives,
tug forelock and kowtow
to a goddess not lovely Britannia,
and even head their religion when
the whole world laughs at them

that country is not worth living in
as their poor will always be feral.
So it's either Quexit
Pexit and Dexit
or
Je'exit this hell of fakes
who fuxits for others.

At a Carnatic Music Concert in Madras

Synthesis of sound by ancient men
who interacted with nature,
restructured molecules from elements
and stringing voices from the land
channelised them into music.
Unveiling vast universes, infinities of spaces
within the haze of our being.

Look! Even the insomniac's eyes are closing.
Palms reflecting rhythm
and reaching for completion.
These are tuftless heads now swaying.

Bare walls of Vani Mahal, Madras
come alive as carved stone
as music covers her lovers like a blanket.
Rain-starred Madras is fresh with jasmine.
this dusk is perpetual.

Diamonds flash like petromax lamps on fair noses
of women moving from one marriage pandal to the next.
Thus the children and the nephews keep leaving
the calendar page where their stars were once marked,
only this music, like the sacred thread,
remains to redress balance
with the ritual of age.

Forty

I become forty with a bang.

First my wife nearly dies and is saved only
by sudden, major surgery
at 12.00 midnight, for
a strangulated,
gangrenous bowel.

Then my father dies.

It takes 18 inches of my wife's bowel,
one for every year
to make me a man.

Taking Breaths

for my Father

I didn't often think of you.
But this summer,
few months before you died
an ordinary medicated shampoo
reminded me of you.

Clean, strong yet vulnerable.

That unique smell of
an asthmatic's inhaler
and air-conditioned office room
where you exercised
a government's power.

A major accident kills hundreds
on that famous line
you built forty years ago.

Then you die alone, clutching
the inhaler in your hand.

One Man's Empire

In the centre of Cavendish Square
was once a statue in stone, of William
the so-called Duke of Cumberland,
riding a white horse,
erected in gratitude
by Lt. General William Strode.

Hundred years later the statue
was removed by the Scots for
his brutality against them
in the battle of Culloden.

The plinth stood empty for many years.
A Korean artist has, in its place,
now made a statue of the same Duke,
both horse and rider in white soap
that will melt in a year or two –
to signify decay inherent in all things -
bodies, lives, reputations.

One man's Empire is
Guantanamo Bay to some
a soap opera to others.

Insignificance

The next time you start your car
do you call it a name?

The next time you go
for a walk do
you call it a name?

The next time you make tea
for a friend
do you call that act by a name?

The next time your dog sneezes
do you call that a name?

Sarah, Gopi, David, Susie are all
just the next
time.

The next time a new galaxy forms
will the Duchess of York
open it with a name?

The next time the Universe dies
Will there be an obituary
in The Times?

Writing a Poem

Like a stranger,
unannounced
you rang my bell.

I didn't know your face,
your colour, your hair,
yet you came knocking
at my door and
I had to let you into the house,
into my head.

You then rearranged the furniture,
hung some new paintings
and left quicker than I thought you would.

The house still looks the same,
but feels cleaner.

Autumn on the Hills of Jouy-en-Josas

Denuded branches,
mellow sun,
afternoon's inexactitude.

Though la Vierge, in gothic flamboyant,
says toujours interdit
art grows.
The observatory predicts a painless day
that mind will step aside
to let the light pass
in the other direction.

Silent spider,
your silver web
splits,
curls
and melts
into the brown shores of autumn.

Condensing on a window pane
is my summer's transparencies,
Delaunay's magic circles,
rude gentleness of a dark haired man
smoking Gitanes.

Jouy-en-Josas, near Versailles, where H.E.C. (Écoles des Hautes Études Commerciales) is located.

Where Kalki Rides

In the petridish at the centre
where Kalki rides
all bacteria die
only truth survives
with the preceptors.

In the next circle most bacteria die
some survive
those who know not
that they know.

The rest wedded
to this demonic world
drift fast to virtual realities,
netherworlds, robotic sex,
love only their selfied
Instagram selves.

Girls glassing each other
drunk in this dreadful pub
they dare call life.

The Destruction of Tripura

From below mid-heaven he gazed, regretfully,
at the blue sky line shimmering
over the golden towers of the magical city.
Just two tears roll from his lustrous eyes onto his cheeks
in pity for those who do not
deserve his punishment, but the others
who are unfazed by the Gods,
dared challenge them and even their existence must die.
Their arrogance tilts the balance of the cosmos.

The city's early warning systems are demonic priests
perpetually incantating mantras of the left handed path.
They sense his purpose and by their power
the city, like a vision in a crystal ball,
is made to disappear.

But only for a moment.
The Lord of the dance is in no mood for games.
He opens his third eye only slightly
and from between just two of its lashes
emerges the nuclear beam to search and destroy.
The edges of the city are barbecued.

Then he raises his brow and
releases the terrible Aghora,
the missile of doom for his enemies.
The city goes in to flames and razed to ashes
falls like a burnt firecracker
into the abyss of space.

The souls of those who worship him
reach him as a little blister on his trigger finger.
The others, the evil ones, enter his bowel
as excreta of the cosmic one to remain there
until another kalpa.
That was a million years ago.

This is another time, another yuga.
Now there are over a thousand Tripuras
puffed up with pride, their hollow leaders
and media heroes manipulating the minds
of those who once worshipped him.

In this age of Kali it is Kalki who
bears the weapons of Shiva riding his faithful white horse.
From his tongue and his hands
emerge the blazing fires of Armagedon.
Unlike Shiva, Kalki sheds no tears.
His face has a thousand masks.
His weapons are secret.
There is no early warning. Save this.
He now takes aim.

Tamasic.

Tamasic attributes: Pleasure seeking.

Tamasic people are driven primarily by their basic instincts -
the desires of the body and the mind seeking pleasure
for their senses through drink, sex, drugs and luxury
with less spiritual or intellectual aspiration.
The Tamasic nature can be violent and can
engage in physical acts of violence or cruelty,
even if incited by others.
These are the equivalent of the thugs on the
periphery of some political parties and teams.
They tend to be most loyal to their friends, family
and country and though their vision of humanity
is narrow and driven by primal needs,
they can transcend this world of Maya through
penance, pilgrimage and retreat.

Definitions of Terror

To behead an innocent man is demonic,
whether for religion or in war.
So is abduction, rape of women or men.

To kill a crowd of people with bombs or
Kalashnikovs in the hope of going to heaven
by decree of any religion is terror,
horrific evil and sheer madness.
No staircase to heaven and sex with sixteen virgins.

To sell arms to a country,
then create a fake war with its neighbour,
killing millions of men, women and children
to sell even more weapons,
is even more horrific, wicked and evil.

To subvert a sovereign country, create a revolution
to take over oil fields, diamonds, gas or minerals,
are acts of demonic countries, evil politicians
bent upon power and wealth for themselves,
their families, their accursed race.

To manufacture viruses, bacteria for insidious invasion,
soldiers pretending to be doctors, priests, humanitarian
relief, is the path paved to eternal hell for the perpetrator.
So many leaders and countries now queueing on this path.
I count them as they pass.
So far, far, far away from
non duality of Brahman.
Foolish man, take Buddha's path.

Stop this War

for All Warmongers

Manufacturing fake pandemics,
'democratic' revolutions
and footage of false attacks
is the unintelligent, White demonic West's
new way of destroying our world,
as they repeatedly did
to my ancestors, Aztecs, the Incas,
Africans and Indians, all over this planet.

Don't lecture others, pretend world leadership
when you are nothing.
Be humble, learn from your past policy
'grab, brutalise and kill'.

Is this Parliament of crows
waiting for distribution of offal?

Lucifer, I command you,
please sit still.

Drop your guns before you take us all to hell –
where I will see you exult in chains.

The VicTory Party

Psoriasis, Fungus and Lichenplanus
met for tea to celebrate each one's
victory as an MP.
Fungus said
"I am raring to go and eat
all parks and trees".
Psoriasis said
"Don't be a fool, come with me,
we must eat human rights,
migrants and damned refugees".
Lichenplanus,
irritated immensely said
"Listen to me - we really must finish
the job given us three
by Party High Command and feed
on doctors, nurses and patients
treated free".
The three fight over their plan
vehemently then finally agree
to finish their tasks and join
Cross Bee, master of media's Streptococci
before the big feast on those with benefits,
blasted unions and rail employees.
Oh! Politics!
Where are the charms
pure egotists see in thy face?
Better dwell between Magdalene's arms
than be ruled by media mace.

Then Spain, now Iraq

Sergio Hidalgo, Spanish aristocrat
once told me how
Alhambra, Toledo, Granada, even Algebra,
all that was good about Spain
came from the Moors,
mostly destroyed in Crusades
except Algebra which
the West quickly claimed.

The same now in Iraq,
Baghdad reduced to rubble
in Bush and Blair's
'Christian War'
now just a B and B
for occupying armies of
a new yet ancient regime of
neo-colonisers.

Sumerian artefacts
looted and sold cheap
to New York's socialites
serving slices of ill-educated,
histories of Euphrates
with canapés.

An Indian Fashion Show

Haughty,
with an adopted, vacant look
in her unintelligent eyes
her hips sway electrically
as though possessed –
like a village oracle in a head-dress
who at least helps the poor
drive away the sorcerers.

She, simply sells brands of beer
to the city's social climbers
who delude themselves
they are part of some invisible
'globalised elite of fashionistas'
and indigenous incarnations of
pretend Armanis,
strutting with dyed hair.

For her it is a passport
to Bolly, Molly, Tolly or Kollywood.
Below the ramp
a pot-bellied producer sits salivating
as bare, bony shoulders twitch
alongside other aspiring models
who think
"I should be up there, not you,
upstart bitch!"

Indian Socialites

Three hundred socialites
waiting to be interviewed.
Three hundred million human beings
waiting for a meal.

This 'contemporary couple' once boasted
of imported cars and hi-fis,
attended clubs and balls
where they danced to music
they did not quite understand.

Now they subtly drop the name
of Yves St. Laurent,
mention friends on the continent
and talk pidgin French.
'passée', come 'coucher avec moi' etc.

Their only claim to fame is the photograph
with a younger leader,
the husband's advertising budget,
Scotch, and the wife's exposed navel
does the rest,
buying fame in pages.

Three hundred socialites
waiting to be interviewed.
Three hundred million human beings
waiting for a meal.

NATO Foreign Policy

Arms for Nato
alms for the Third World
bombs for Nato
buns for the rest.

U.S. Foreign Policy

Today's puppet
tomorrow's monster

Today's arms buyer
tomorrow's dictator,

Today's demon
tomorrow's ally.

International Community.

A few cheap Whiteys meet over tea
and call themselves
'The International Community'.

"Let's create a no fly zone over Iraq,
let's bomb the shit out of their schools,
hospitals and libraries,
get their children amputated
so we can offer tea and sympathy, after all
we are the International Community of thugs,
the best protection racket
armed with drones and nuclear.

Then we will play puppetry
with the next regime."

Iraq is done and dusted.
Huge commissions pocketed
by Whitey politicians and
CIA controlled media 'embedded'.

"Next let's move to Libya –
let's bomb the shite out of Benghazi,
after a beer and a curry."
And so it goes.

British Values

Let them eat Formula 1,
let them eat Tour de France,
let them eat our great Olympic Spirit,
let them eat Parades at Horse Guards,
but let them not eat bread.

We gentlemen don't have soup at lunch.
Let them eat soup all day from our soup kitchens.

Let them marvel at the house
we built for Gloriana Barge,
let them gawp at Buck House,
let them see our Heritage homes,
but let them not have a room to sleep in
let them squat in spare bedrooms of pensioners.

Let them learn 'British Values'
taught in great schools of Magaluf.
Let them "Rejoice, Rejoice" in the victories
of their leaders but let them not know
of the millions in commissions we earned
from arms and oil deals,
NOT from speeches.

Let them understand all except us are radicalised,
devils not C of E / Holy See.
That all other countries are Hell.

That God is an Englishman.
That our Bishops now menstruate
oil and natural gas
for further cooking up Faith.

Let them learn that 'B' means only Britain,
'G' means Great, 'E' Empire
and 'P' our national pastime of Pædophilia.
Let them learn to sext but let them not learn
the other letters of the alphabet from A to Z -
or how to speak.
Let them have gastric bands
leading to post-operative adhesions,
and intestinal obstructions
for surgery on trollies.
Let them buy their medicines
cheap on the internet –
not free prescriptions,
let them queue for months for their GPs.
Let their old die on Liverpool pathways –
while ours survive in Harley St.

For we are the Chavs and the Celebs –
they are hungry and will eat us one day.

A Brat is Born.

A rat is born chewing
yet again at the self-respect
of poor Englishmen.

Like the leper seeking alms
pushes his deformed limb
in tourists' faces,
the British with nothing left,
push their Royals,
ugly stump of a diseased Empire
on their citizens, still called subjects
of royal rats and monkeys.

Grate Britain

Outside the grey sky hangs like a dirty tea towel
from the boarding-houses of Bayswater.
Everyone in this city is a pimp
or a prostitute. They sell their image, titles, or
the poor ones, most honest of all,
the holes in their bodies.
A shopkeeper's daughter from Grantham
has privatised their souls.

A yuppy redevelops and rents
his wife's anus to City Corp
for an enormous sum.
"Deconstruction!
A major new architectural phenomenon!"
says the pseud.
"How wonderful!" says the Party,
"Isn't Britain booming beyond our
wildest expectations!".

Outside the cold bites hard.
The cardboard city grows.

Transmigration Desk

As of today
18th April 2009 at 9.25pm
the sky is officially closed
to all immigration.
There will be no more souls
let through
into the firmament.

No politicians, celebrities,
reality show contestants
or P.R. girls.

All will remain
on Earth till a new Shiva
comes dredging,
and Bhagiratha wills
Akasha Ganga to flow on his locks.

Andrew Green, poor sod
"watches" immigration!
Our offices are now closed
flooded with souls
denied transmigration.

There are no more
bogeys left on this platform.
Only bogeys of lives won or lost.
The whine not of wheels but of the souls
between death and liberation.

Then the dying, uncertain
on which platform
their train is meant to be.

The Good, the Sad and the Ugly

Self uploading
selfie taking
twitter loving
Facebook driven trolls,

boob expanding
bum extending
botox ridden
buttock selling dolls,

bomb dropping
drone sending
missile trading,
hedge funding,
millions making,
children killing,
power loving,
politician,
man,

the bells of seven hells now toll for you.

Not with glee
but great sadness
I watch half of mankind fall
into mutant driven halls
of nether worlds.

Further Reviews:

" The play written by Gopi Warrier tackles the huge divide between Western values, ideas about medicine, spirituality and the lack of it in the West, racism, poetry, love and philosophy. Gopi Warrier manages to weave all this into wonderful poetry which makes you want to catch and linger on every word."
Linda Bilgorri- on 'Godsports' at New End Theatre

"An underlying message of Gopi Warrier's work is the need to preserve the religious, cultural and philosophical traditions of India and the absence of roots amongst the upper-middleclass Indians
sadly stuck in the vicious cycle of materialistic fulfilment."
Deccan Herald, Bangalore, India

"The core message of Gopi Warrier's work is the need to preserve the philosophical and spiritual traditions of India that have evolved over millennia. He smoothly breaks the Hindu- Muslim barrier and stereotypes with his plays and poetry." *Asian Age, Mumbai*

"Gopi Warrier lives in London and has lived in and travelled around the world. He has a facile pen for satire, eye for the shape of language and a sensitive ear for cadence. One of the best poems in the collection "Three Travellers" talks of others who "sped towards the mirage"
while the three travellers "walk from the promised land"
Keki Daruwalla, leading Indian poet writing in the Hindusthan Times on Gopi Warrier's first collection of poems "In a Country near Zimbabwe"

"Gopi Warrier's genius is the synthesis of Eastern and Western Mythologies."
The Hindustan Times

"Author Gopi Warrier clearly understands the logic of asset stripping and endemic corruption in the city. I particularly enjoyed Sarah Hall's crystal sharp Rodean Vowels and Lloyd Morris' swagger as the deals dodgy facilitator "
" Ego of the Yogis" is a regretful and romantic invocation of the search for true love and of the contamination of yoga in the western world "

Reviews in Remote Goat of Gopi Warrier's plays "Polyester Lordship" and "Ego of the Yogis"